To The Moon, and to Saturn, and Everything in Between

AJ Valentine

BookLeaf Publishing

Presentation by *BookLeaf Publishing*

Web: www.bookleafpub.com

E-mail: info@bookleafpub.com

ISBN: 9789357612531

First edition 2022

DEDICATION

To My Gran

ACKNOWLEDGEMENT

Diane Fitzgerald for funding my participation

Maya Angelou, Edgar Allen Poe, Shel Silverstein, and Taylor Swift for helping me find my writing style

Seven - Taylor Swift for inspiring this book

When I'm Sixty-Four - The Beatles

American Pie - Don McLean

PREFACE

Life isn't about doing the best you can to do the best you can. It's about living authentically, finding happiness, and doing whatever the hell it is you want.

3 A.M.

I wake up at 3 A.M. almost every night
I can't seem to sleep anymore
My mind is always in fight or flight
I get up and make a palette on the floor
Staring blankly at the ceiling I begin to think
When did this happen to me?
Is this the way it will always be?
The lovers love with everything they have
And the dreamers are the ones that get to dream
We're taught to be neither
The moment we're able to think
By 18 you must know precisely who you are and
everything you want
I don't know who I am
Or what I want
Isn't that what this life is for?
So, for now, I'll just close my eyes
And try to get some sleep on this palette in the
middle of the floor

Hitting R.E.M.

To be truly alive
Is to feel like you're dreaming
Sitting on cloud 9
Floating past the mountains
As The Sun walks on home in the west
The colors have never been more vibrant
than this dusk
It's more effervescent than the rest
As bubbles start to form at my ears
I look out to the air-brushed sky
And think if this is how living truly were
I'd stay on this cloud for 1000 light-years

Astronaut

What if I were an astronaut?
My first mission: Artemis 17
Flying to Saturn and stopping by The Moon on
my way back
No need for a rocket
I constructed wings from feathers and wax
I won't fly too close to the Sun
It's the opposite direction in fact
I prepare myself for takeoff
Readying myself to fly
I lift myself up off the ground and into the
beautiful night sky
I think I might just be an astronaut
Because I have never been quite this high
The Big Dipper is there
Here
Right In front of my eyes

A letter in the sky with diamonds

Swinging on a cumulus
Counting the stars
I see a mailbox on a cloud not too far from Mars
With a tiny package inside or a letter, possibly a
card
I pump my legs faster and faster
Swinging over to that cloud bordering Deimos
The smallest moon of Mars
I grab the contents out of the mailbox
Contemplating if this was right
I've always been the nosey type
I must know what's inside!
I untie the bow, take it off, and open up a corner
Sneaking my right hand inside
In it are a notepad, pencil, and a paintbrush too
with a note reading
"I'll see you very soon"
Addressed
To: Me
From: My friend The Moon

To: The Moon

Dear Moon,
You're my only friend
The only companion I have when the fake
smiles are worn out
And I can't sleep
When the day comes to an overwhelming end
I put it in an envelope and lick the stamp
Sending love notes to The Moon
But I haven't met her yet

And to Saturn

I have a map in one hand and my gifts in the
other
Setting off to Saturn
First stopping at Jupiter and Mars

Seven or Seventy

Let kids be kids
Even when they're adults
Riding carousels
Jumping in the mud
Chasing their friends until the street lights come
on

6th Grade

Shoes during recess running on the grass
School bells ringing dismissing you from class
The smell of fresh baked cookies during a winter
storm
And the taste of pure bliss on a cone in the heat
of The Sun
When you're busy doing nothing but having
some fun

Mars

I bet you can't imagine what's on Mars
Did you know they had all-terrain helicars
And purple space people with heads twice the
size of ours
On the surface of Mars
There are dinosaurs that play bass banjo guitars
And they sell chocolate chip carrot cakes out of
little mason jars
All the way out here on planet Mars

October 31st, 2013

A long long time ago
I can still remember how everything used to
make me smile
Playing make-believe and dress up
We'd sing and play and dance
With glow-in-the-dark wands in our hands
When everyone was happy for awhile

Flying through the Asteroid Belt

Rocks the size of cities hurdling from every
which way
I hesitate to power through
Facing my fears
I imagine they are all jelly beans
And fly straight through
My wings come out unscathed, untattered,
unscarred
All 9000 feathers still in place
I come upon the largest thing I've ever seen
With a great red dot three miles under her spleen

Jupiter

This one is my favorite
The fifth from The Sun
Beauty is her name
Grace her age
Go tell it on the mountain
Where the moons always shine
And the sun never sets

Thirteen

The unluckiest number
The one they skip on elevator floors
Going from 12 to 14
Changing everything
Too old for this
But too young for that
Not knowing what any of this is for

Catwalking on Saturn's Rings

Please picture me on the rings
I hit my peak at 17
Feet in the sea of eternity
I never knew what I wanted
Now I'm high in the sky
With a galaxy under me
There are still beautiful things

Celestial Magic

Arnold Palms in the summer
I paint some art
On the notepad I got from queen mother
And though we can't stay here for long
I'll always be there for you
Your rings glow like a lantern
Now I must go to The Moon from Saturn

No, not mine... URS!

Leaving Saturn but I'm not ready to head back
yet
I fly a little way to the Seventh planet
The one whose name makes me giggle like a
little kid would when they hear it
What a funny name for a giant piece of ice
floating in the abyss!
I'll forever think of that particular anatomy
Well, how can I not?
The word is right there in the name
But if I weren't all alone out here I'd be ridiculed
and called immature
For laughing at a word that everyone does
When they're all alone
But, growing up means being serious
And tough and stern
In that case
I think growing up is overrated
And dare I say overdone

When I'm 34

When I get older
Thirteen years from now
Will you be sending me love letters
Birthday greetings a bottle of wine
If you get bored
Would you walk out the door
Will you love me, will you still hold me
When I'm 34

The Theatre Multiverse

We were born to play
A natural tendency that should never go away
So, put on your character shoes and best
ensemble costumes
Turn down the house lights
Cue Curtains
As the Universe proudly presents
"What is the Meaning of Life?"

In the Light of the Midnight Sun

My pencil swift as a knife
Cutting you deeper with every word
Each syllable pierces through your heart like a
stake
As day breaks through the stratosphere
Killing Nosferatu where she stands

Oh My God I'm on The Moon!

My last stop before I head home
Diana herself
The great full moon
One small step for me and one large step for an
ant
I place down my bedazzled flag
To stand on my tip toes
And look to my right
There is Venus and Mercury too
And a total eclipse of The Sun
Its red burnt orange hue
I can almost smell the fire of passion running
through her heart
I take out my paintbrush and try to capture the
essence of this cosmic art

And Everything in Between

This was a needed journey
I've never needed anything more
My heart went Supernova
I can't wait to see what else is in store
I fly toward the room on the top floor
Climbing through the window
I take my wings off and hang them on a hook on
the door
I sit on my bed to ponder the experience
And wake up on that palette in the middle of my
bedroom floor